A Handbook For The
CLARKE®
TIN WHISTLE

By Bill Ochs

The Pennywhistler's Press

Acknowledgements

Many people have helped with this small book and tape, more than can be acknowledged here. I would especially like to thank the Clarke Tinwhistle Company as well as: Dick Bagwell, Tony Barrand, Mr. E. Button, Keith Chandler, Mr. F.S. Clarke, Peter Cooke, Caleb Crowell, Margaret De Motte, Jerry Epstein, Anne Humpherys, Terry Hunt, Jeremy Montagu, Joe Pecnik, Bill Rowen, John Sarney, Robert Sheldon, and William White.

For permission to use tunes, the following collectors, composers, arrangers and publishers:

Marshall Barron, *Rufty Tufty* from *The Geud Man of 55th Street*, (Playford Consort Publications)

Samuel Bayard, *Johnny Get Your Haircut* from *Hill Country Tunes*, (American Folklore Society) and *Governor King's March* from *Dance To the Fiddle, March To The Fife* (Penn State U. Press)

The Colonial Williamsburg Foundation, *The Boston March* (arr. John C. Moon) from *Musick Of The Fifes And Drums*, Vol.I

Norman Maclean, *Cion A'Bhuntàta/Scarce O'Tatties*

Ossian Publications, *The Cat's Jig* from *Wallflower* by Bill Meek

Raymond Ward for his father's composition, *Jim Ward's Jig*

Musicians whose playing has been a source of inspiration as well as a source of some of the tunes in this book: Mary Bergin, Willie Clancy, Michael Crehan, Séamus Ennis, Tommy Makem, Cathal McConnell, Josie McDermot, Tom McHaile, Mickey McNicholas, Paddy Moloney, Donncha Ó Briain, Seán Potts, Micho Russell, Michael Tubridy and others.

My music teachers Andy Conroy, Pat Mitchell and Tom Standeven.

My music students who kindly allowed their teacher a brief "sabbatical" to finish this project.

The musicians who joined me on the tape: Tony Bloch, Patricia Brady, Lisa Gutkin, Ben Harms and John Sarney.

The production people, working with whom has been a pleasure and education for me: Norman Forsythe, music copyist; Jeremy Harris, recording engineer; Charles Kreloff, cover design; Peggy Lyons and the staff of Jetsetters Cold Type, typesetting and mechanicals; Lynn Pantuso, layout, design and making order of chaos.

Finally, my friend Wayne Kirn, who designed the format and whose help really got this project off the ground; and my parents, Herb and Betsy Ochs, who supported the project in innumerable ways.

Third Printing, March 1990

ISBN 0-9623456-0-1

Published by The Pennywhistler's Press,
P.O. Box 2473, New York, N.Y. 10108

Introduction

The Clarke tin whistle is a remarkable survival. Hand made in England of rolled tinplate with a wooden fipple plug, this same instrument was played by street musicians in Charles Dickens' time.

For many years, especially in rural Ireland, the Clarke was *the* tin whistle — the only kind there was. The instrument has a dedicated and loyal following of people who grew up with it.

My introduction to the Clarke tin whistle came through listening to Tommy Makem of the group *The Clancy Brothers And Tommy Makem* in the early 1960's. He played it with the verve of a fife or piccolo and I was immediately hooked.

Later I met old men from the west of Ireland who played in a totally different style. Their fingers seemed to dance and flutter over the holes, producing an endless stream of warbling birdsong. This was not the rousing sound of a fife, but a subtle and complicated interlace decorated with little turns called *"rolls"*.

These rolls and other ornaments sound particularly effective on a Clarke tin whistle. The instrument has a robust ring to it as well as a bite and responsiveness that organ makers call *"chiff"*. This is a result of the configuration of the Clarke mouthpiece and conical bore, which also gives the whistle a "flutey" lower octave.

In our time many people play the modern plastic-tipped tin whistle, a good instrument with a light, relatively clear tone. In my opinion, the Clarke and the modern whistle are almost two different instruments and should be approached as such — repertoire which brings out the beauty of one may not do justice to the other and vice versa.

I've tried to select tunes for this book which suit the Clarke and take advantage of its unique timbre. Much of the advanced music is from Ireland, reflecting the fact that tin whistle playing has flourished in that country and developed into an art form. There are also selections from England, Scotland, and the U.S. which illustrate different aspects of the instrument's musical personality.

The format of the book has been designed with the hope that anyone who picks it up will find something geared to his or her level of musical ability and interest. Of necessity this entailed compromises. It is not possible to say everything, but this should at least get you pointed in the right direction. Happy whistling!*

*N.B. I've decided to treat the Clarke C whistle as a transposing instrument and write the music in D and related keys. There are historical and practical reasons for this which are explained in the appendix on page 77.

THE CLARKE TINWHISTLE COMPANY

The Clarke Tinwhistle Company was founded by Robert Clarke, who was born in the tiny English farming village of Coneyweston, Suffolk in 1816.

As a young man he worked as a farm laborer. During very rainy seasons the farmer with whom he had hired would cut Clarke's wages. These were only nine shillings a week in the best of times, not much for a married man.

But Clarke was a person of some musical ability and so decided to try his hand at making tin whistles. He fashioned the necessary tools with the help of the local blacksmith and began to produce whistles in or about the year 1843.

The population of Coneyweston at that time was just 250 people. To find a large enough market for his whistles, Clarke loaded his tools and wares onto a handcart and took to the road, selling whistles along the way wherever he stopped.

The 1851 census lists him as a "hawker" and as being absent from home. It is not known exactly what his rounds were, but he is said to have at one point pushed his handcart all the way from Barningham in Suffolk to the city of Manchester in Lancashire, a distance of 150 miles.

Manchester was a large manufacturing center with ready access to transportation and raw materials. It offered Clarke an excellent base from which to expand his trade, so he decided to move his family there sometime between 1851 and 1858. He built two cottages with a small factory at back. Eventually he was employing fifteen people and had established a reputation as being the largest manufacturer of tin whistles in England.

Yet the company remained very much a small cottage industry. Machines were used to cut the wooden plugs and tinplate as well as pierce the holes in the whistles, but all other operations were done by hand. Clarke worked side by side with his sons who followed him into the trade, as did succeeding generations of the family.

With the exception of wartime and a brief reorganizational period, the whistles have been in continuous production by the Clarke Company from circa 1843 to the present.

The Clarke tin whistle of today retains all the essential features of those manufactured by Robert Clarke in the mid-19th century. The instrument is still made of tinplate with a wooden end plug. Delicate operations continue to be done by hand and most importantly, the traditional conical bore has been retained to give the instrument its unique tone and timbre. Some modern materials, such as a non-toxic epoxy resin, have been introduced for a more durable and lasting finish.

HISTORY OF THE TIN WHISTLE

The tin whistle seems to have been a relatively new instrument when Robert Clarke started making them in the 1840's. The earliest literary reference to the instrument is from 1825. It is probably somewhat older than this, but perhaps not much. Tinplate only first became readily and cheaply available in 1785 at the beginning of the industrial revolution.

Of course the tin whistle had many antecedents made of different materials that go back a bit further than 1785. A flute made of animal bone discovered in a cave in France is believed to be 25,000 years old!

Bone flutes were quite common in Europe through the Middle Ages. Some of these were of the whistle variety, also known as *fipple flutes*. Fipple is an old word for the plug that partially seals the end of the flute in which the windway is located. This windway directs the air stream against a cutting edge or blade which causes the air to vibrate and produce sound.

Other instruments in the fipple flute family are the eight-holed *recorder*, developed around the 15th century, and its close relative, the six-holed *flageolet*. Both these instruments were generally made of wood and turned on a lathe. At some stage it was discovered that an inexpensive substitute for the wooden flageolet could be made by rolling a sheet of tinplate around a mandrel. The instrument was called the *tin flageolet*, *tin flute*, or the name by which we know it today, the *tin whistle*.

In our time one most often associates the tin whistle with Irish music. However evidence suggests that the instrument was well known in England, America and to some extent, Scotland. It seems to have once been a very common household instrument, as popular and ubiquitous as the harmonica.

The following letter from one J.M Wayne to the famous Long Island painter William Sidney Mount attests to the tin whistle's popularity in mid-19th century America:

New York
January 26, 1868

Sir,

......I would be very much obliged if you would buy me another tin whistle and send it up by Fanny Seabury whom Miss Maria said was coming up to the city the latter part of this week. Those whistles are very much in demand here now, and some of the little boys have the old kind but there are two or three notes false in each one of them. I can play almost any tune on mine now learning them all by ear...*

Despite its popularity, very little has been written about the tin whistle, probably because it was generally considered a toy. By far the most interesting document related to its history is an interview from Volume III of Henry Mayhew's *London Labour And The London Poor*.** In 1856 the journalist Mayhew took down an "oral history" from a young tin whistler who made his living playing in the streets and pubs of London. The piece reads as though out of Dickens.

THE STORY OF WHISTLING BILLY

The son of a London barber, Whistling Billy ran away from home at the age of 12. He fell in with a few "mates" who happened to be petty thieves. This association landed him in jail where he had all his hair cut off and was forced to live on dry bread and gruel. On his release he was given a shilling, purchased a tin whistle, and began to play on the street.

At that time he knew six tunes, but eventually worked his repertoire up to fifty pieces and added dancing while playing the whistle to his act. He danced the hornpipe and the jig, the latter which he could perform with his toes turned in as if he were bowlegged. One of his other comic turns was to play the whistle in his nose, which he could do quite effectively except when he had a cold.

At harvest time he would make an annual tour of the south of England to play for harvest suppers and dances. Some of these dances were held by moonlight, with Whistling Billy mounted on a haywagon or perched on a pile of straw piping away to as many as forty people at a time. He was well looked after by the haymakers, who treated him as a welcome guest.

His brief narrative is at times quite humorous, at other times touching. A few points of historical interest emerge from it. For one, Whistling Billy mentions Clarke by name and cites him as being the largest "manufactory" of tin whistles at the time. He also alludes to two earlier makers of whistles — someone named Swinden and an anonymous maker who preceded Swinden.

Both Whistling Billy and Mayhew refer to the instrument interchangeably as a tin whistle and a pennywhistle which leads to the question of the origin of the name *pennywhistle*.

* Collection of the Museums at Stony Brook, N.Y.
** q.v., pp. 199-204

DID THE PENNYWHISTLE EVER COST A PENNY?

At one stage in his career Whistling Billy actually sold whistles on the street. He charged twopence each for them and sometimes got as much as sixpence or a shilling. But he only paid threepence a dozen wholesale for the whistles — *that's 1/4 penny each!*

At this price other merchants were probably quite content to sell them for a penny or even a half a penny (a *"ha' penny"*). There is evidence that Robert Clarke may have made a whistle that sold for half a penny. One of his earlier models was called a *"Meg"*, a Lancashire schoolboys' term for ha'penny.

It would have been the normal course of business for the price to have reached the penny level at some point, which would seem to explain the origin of the term pennywhistle. Yet there is another theory.

In some places there was a custom of *giving a penny* to a child or street musician who was heard playing the whistle. Some people claim that this practice accounts for the name pennywhistle and perhaps they are partially right.

More than likely the instrument was first called a pennywhistle when it actually could be purchased for a penny. As the price rose the old name probably just stuck. Subsequent generations may have invented the custom of giving a penny to a musician to make sense of retaining the name in the face of rising "inflation".

THE TIN WHISTLE IN MODERN TIMES

The tin whistle has enjoyed a great renewal of popularity in the last 25 years with the revival of interest in folk music. Modern sound technology in both the concert hall and recording studio allows the whistle to be highlighted and emerge as a solo instrument in ways it never could have before. Irish music groups such as The Clancy Brothers and Tommy Makem, The Dubliners, Sean Ó Ríada's Ceoltóirí Chualann (which later became the Chieftains) and of course the classical flutist James Galway can all share some of the credit for raising the stature of the instrument in the public eye and introducing many listeners to its charms for the first time.

As a result more and more people are playing the whistle themselves and it is once again becoming a truly ubiquitous instrument.

ABOUT TRADITIONAL MUSIC

Most of the tunes in this book have been passed down orally from one generation of folk musician to the next through what is called the *folk process*. The original composers are generally not known and the tunes are often transformed as they are handed on. Dozens of different versions may exist of a particular tune and no one way of playing it is looked on as "the right way". Sometimes a tune may even have several different names or one name may attach itself to several different tunes.

Such is the nature of the folk process. Music that has been shaped by this process is often called *traditional music*.

LESSONS

How To Use This Book

The beginning lessons are designed to introduce you to some of the rudiments of music one step at a time. Only such music theory as is necessary to play the type of tunes in this book is included. The emphasis is on listening and doing.

If you are new to learning music, a few things are very important to remember. *Don't play the tunes fast until you can play them perfectly at a slow speed.* Rushing tends to cause mistakes which are difficult to unlearn.

For best results practice regularly. Even a small amount of practice every day is preferable to large amounts from time to time.

Listen to the tape as much as possible. In this way you will absorb the music by ear, a time-honored practice amongst traditional folk musicians. Some of the best tin whistle players I've heard don't read a note of music.

On the other hand, many people are needlessly put off by musical notation. Learning the names of the notes on the staff is accessible to anyone who can read this sentence. (We are just talking about seven letters of the alphabet and a few lines and spaces.) The subtleties of rhythm take a bit more understanding, but here you have the tape as a resource to help you.

Experiment to find the style of learning that best suits you.

The tunes basically get more difficult as the book goes along — in places there are some fairly big jumps for which you may not be ready. In this case I would encourage you to supplement your learning with other tin whistle books. Some excellent ones are listed in the bibliograhy.

NOTE

All Clarke whistles are tested for playability before leaving the factory. Because they are hand made out of largely malleable material, the tone, volume, degree of "chiff", etc. can vary from one instrument to another. These differences are considered normal. Several different Clarke whistles, both old and new, have been used on the tape that accompanies this book.

Experienced Clarke players often pry and pinch the tin of the mouthpiece to make personal adjustments to their instruments. For instance, by pressing down on the top of the windway, the amount of air required to play the whistle can be reduced.

It is not recommended that beginners attempt this delicate procedure. Going too far can adversely affect the tone of the whistle. It would be best to learn some tunes first and get to know your instrument as it is.

Getting Started

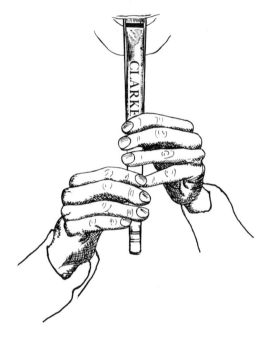

The most important thing to concentrate on from the start is covering the holes completely so that no air leaks or escapes from under the fingers. Leakage of air will cause squeaks, as well as poor pitch and tone.

The best method of sealing the holes airtight is to:

1. COVER THE HOLES WITH THE PADS OF THE FINGERS, NOT THE TIPS. (The pad is the area about midway between the tip and the first joint.)
2. HOLD THE FINGERS FLAT: DO NOT ARCH OR CURVE THEM.

(Refer often to the drawing above for the correct finger position.)

First Notes

Let's begin by just covering one hole. Place the thumb of the left hand behind the top hole of the whistle. (That's the one closest to the name CLARKE.) Cover that hole with the pad of the index finger of the left hand. (We'll call this finger "left one" or L1 for short.)

Blow gently and steadily to sound the note B.

Leave the thumb and index finger where they are. Cover the next hole with the pad of the middle finger of your left hand (L2), and blow gently to sound the note A.

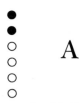

Leaving those fingers where they are, cover the third hole with the pad of the left ring finger (L3). So with the top three holes covered air tight, blow gently to sound the note G.

The three notes you've just sounded spell the word **"BAG."** Remember this word and you'll have memorized your first three notes.

Practice these notes on your own and then try the following exercise.

G   A   B   A   B   A   G   G   B   A   B   G   G

Tonguing

Suppose you have to play a passage with a lot of identical notes all in row. How would you separate them?

By whispering the syllable "too" or "tuh" into the whistle, you can separate the notes very clearly.

This is called *tonguing* because the tongue flicks gently and inaudibly when you pronounce these syllables. Try using the tongue to articulate the notes in the following example.

G   G   G   G   A   A   A   A   B   B   A   A   G   G

For the present, tongue each note in all the pieces you play. At a later stage you will learn a different way of playing.

Now let's try a simple tune. It's a variant of *Mary Had A Little Lamb.* Remember to tongue each note.

MERRILY WE ROLL ALONG

Traditional

Practice the tune slowly at first.
Don't stop the breath between each note.
Breathe as you would if you were singing the song.

Sometimes with repeated playing, the whistle mouthpiece may become filled with moisture. To clear it, place your finger over the rectangular slot just below the mouthpiece and blow forcibly.

Three More Notes

The next three notes are the lowest on the whistle. It is important to blow them gently or else your sound will "jump" into the instrument's higher register. Concentrate on producing soft, mellow tones.

Put your fingers in position for playing G and cover the next open hole with the pad of the index finger of the right hand (R1).

Place the right thumb under the whistle in a comfortable position below this finger. (*Don't use the left pinky to cover the hole. This should be curled back slightly to keep it out of the way.*) With four holes covered, blow gently to sound the note F sharp (written F#).

F#

Leaving those fingers in position, cover the next hole with the pad of your right middle finger (R2). Blow gently to sound the note E.

E

Finally cover the last hole with the right ring finger (R3) and blow gently to sound the note D.

D

The fingers of the right hand spell the word **FED**.

So now you have **BAG** & **FED**. Remember these two words and you've practically memorized the entire scale.

Practice F#, E, & D on your own.

Play the following.

D E F# E   F# E D   D F# E F#   D   D

Once you know the notes F#, E, & D try the next tune.

TWINKLE, TWINKLE LITTLE STAR

Traditional

D D A A   B B A   G G F# F#   E E D

A A G G   F# F# E   A A G G   F# F# E

D D A A   B B A   G G F# F#   E E D

Choose a tempo at which you can play without making any mistakes, even if it seems artificially slow. Speed will develop gradually.

It is also important to hold your fingers close to the whistle when they're not actually covering a hole — about 1/2 to 3/4″ from the instrument is a good guideline. The less distance the fingers have to travel, the easier it is to find the holes and develop agility.   13

Practice Tunes

The following tunes use all the notes you've learned so far.

LONDON BRIDGE

children's song   English

A   B   A   G   F# G A   E F# G   F# G   A

A   B   A   G   F# G A   E   A   F# D

In this next piece there are two musical symbols for you to learn.

BREATH MARK

,

The *breath mark*
(apostrophe) suggests
where you might
breathe.

REPEAT SIGNS

Repeat signs mean to
repeat the music between
the two signs. If there
is only one repeat sign
return to the beginning.

AU CLAIR DE LA LUNE
(By The Light Of The Moon)

folksong   French

G   G   G   A   B   A   G   B   A   A   G

A   A   A   A   E   E   A   G   F# E   D

G   G   G   A   B   A   G   B   A   A   G

Completing The Scale

With just two more notes you'll have a full scale. Look at the finger diagram for the note C Sharp (written C#).

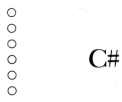

All the holes are uncovered. Try playing this note and you may find that the whistle goes flying out of your mouth onto the floor! The thumbs alone will not suffice to hold the instrument.

To play C# it is necessary to use a BALANCE FINGER. Many people find that the best method of balancing the instrument is to *cover* the lowest hole of the whistle with the ring finger of the right hand (R3). Covering this hole does not affect the pitch of the note.

Other people balance the whistle with the pinky of the right hand placed in the area below the lowest hole where the decorative gold bands are.

Choose the method which is most comfortable for you and which does not move your other fingers out of alignment.

Practice the note C#. Hopefully the whistle did not fall out of your mouth!

The next note to learn is middle D. (What you already know is low D.) It is fingered with all the holes covered except the top one. You may need to blow slightly harder to sound this note.

Now try to play the scale from low D to middle D (designated like this: D′).

| D | E | F# | G | A | B | C# | D′ |

It is helpful to use your balance finger for *all* upper hand notes — G through C#. This not only stabilizes the instrument, but also keeps your fingers from straying too far from the holes.

Once you can play up the scale, try going down.

| D′ | C# | B | A | G | F# | E | D |

This is called the D major scale. It begins and ends on D. You now know eight notes or one *octave*.

Here is a new musical symbol which you will encounter in the next tune.

𝄽

This is called a *quarter rest* and indicates a one beat pause or silence.

The following well travelled melody goes by many names. In America it is called *Sweet Betsy From Pike*.

SWEET BETSY FROM PIKE

folksong   American

D		D	F#	A		A	G	E		E	D	D		D		D
D	F#	A		D′	D′	D′		C#	A	A		A		A
D′	D′	D′		C#	A	F#		G	A	B		A		D
D	F#	A		A	G	E		E	D	D		D

The ABC's Of Music

So far you've been playing partially by ear and partially by looking at the letter symbols written in this book. Now is a good time to learn to identify the letter names of the notes for yourself. It is not hard to do.

Music is written on a grid called a *staff.* It has five *lines* and four *spaces.*

Line   Space

If the round part of the note has the line going through it like this, it is on a line.

If the round part of the note is between two lines like this, it is in a space.

The names of the four spaces from bottom to top are:

F   A   C   E

This conveniently spells FACE, an easy way to remember the names of the spaces.

The names of the five lines from bottom to top are:

E   G   B   D   F

To learn the names of the lines, remember the sentence **E**very **G**ood **B**oy **D**oes **F**ine. The first letter of each word identifies the names of the lines.

Low D is the lowest note on the whistle, and the lowest note on the staff:

D

Now write in the notes for the English children's song, *The Muffin Man*. The answers are on page 76 but don't look until after you've tried playing it.

THE MUFFIN MAN

children's song
English

For the remaining nine lessons, the names of the notes for the tunes will be given on page 76 at the back of the book. It is suggested that you use these notes only as a reference and that you make every effort to identify the notes on the staff as they appear in tunes. This will prepare you for the rest of the tunes in the book, for which no note names are given. You may write the notes in for a few more tunes if you wish, but then just try to mentally identify them. This process will be slow at first, but the long term benefits will be well worth the effort.

LESSON TWO

Another New Note: C Natural

In completing the D scale you learned the note C sharp (C♯). There is another C which is also used very frequently on the tin whistle: C natural (C♮). C natural is a half tone lower in pitch than C sharp and it is used in other scales. There are several ways to play C♮. The two most popular methods are explained here.

One way is to leave the top hole of the whistle open and cover the next two holes with the left middle and left ring fingers (L2 & L3). The bottom holes are open, as in the diagram below.

C♮

The other method is to *half cover* the top hole with the left index finger (L1). To learn this technique, first play the note B. Keeping L1 in place, straighten it at the joint closest to the finger tip. This movement should open half of the top hole and produce the note C natural. It takes a bit of practice to get the knack of this.

Choose one method and stick to it for the present. Then try the following exercise.

To tell whether to use C♮ or C♯ in a tune look in the C space (third from bottom) at the beginning of each line of music. If you see a sharp sign in that space, play C sharp. If there is no sharp sign, play C natural.

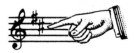

Play C sharp

Play C natural

This short version of the English singing game *Oranges & Lemons* is a good introduction to using C♮ in a tune.

ORANGES & LEMONS

singing game

English

THE LONDON COSTERMONGER.

" Here Pertaters ! Kearots and Turnups ! fine Brockello-o-o ! "

Quarter Notes, Half Notes And Whole Notes

Once you've had a bit of practice identifying notes you will notice different symbols and probably wonder why the same note is written a number of different ways.

These symbols indicate whether a note is to be held long, cut short, or played somewhere in between. To understand exactly how long to play each note, we need to introduce a musical concept called the *beat*.

Did you ever notice how most lively music gets your foot tapping almost automatically? The pulse that you feel is the beat. Each note that you hear gets a certain number of taps or beats.

To illustrate this let's look at the very first tune you learned, *Merrily We Roll Along*. I'll play it again on the tape with a quiet click in the background. Listen to the tune, look at the music, and try to tap your foot in time with the click.

You probably noticed that most of the notes got just one tap of the foot. These are called *quarter notes* and look like this:

There were several notes at the ends of phrases that got two taps. These are called *half notes* and look like this:

Finally there was one long note at the very end of the tune that got four taps. This is called a *whole note* and looks like this:

Rewind the tape and repeat the exercise until you can easily recognize the three types of notes.

Once this is clear to you, here is another musical concept to think about:

Beats are organized into units called *measures*.
Each measure has a specific number of beats.

When music is written the measures are separated by vertical lines called *bar lines*. A *double bar* line indicates the end of a piece of music.

BAR LINE	*BAR LINE*	*BAR LINE*	*DOUBLE BAR LINE*

Go back to *Merrily We Roll Along* and count the number of beats in each individual measure.

In this tune there are four beats per measure. Because of this and the fact that every quarter note gets one beat, the piece is said to be in *Four/Four Time*.

Four/Four is notated like this: **4/4**   This is called a *time signature*.

The top number indicates how many beats per measure.
The bottom number indicates what sort of note gets one beat.

For any time signature with a 4 on the bottom, the note values are the same.

Now let's listen to the Appalachian folksong, *Go Tell Aunt Rhody* to get a feeling for the different note values.

GO TELL AUNT RHODY

folksong   American

Rewind the tape and tap your foot along with the quiet click you hear in the background.

Repeat the exercise while looking at the music. Notice where your foot is tapping once, twice, or four times per note.

Learn the tune and pay special attention to holding the notes just their right length.

Eighth Notes

Eighth notes are found in most lively tunes. These are short little notes that look like this:

Eighth notes have a little "flag" on their stem. When eighth notes occur next to each other in a tune, they are connected by a single bar as shown above.

An eighth note gets half a beat. This means that if you're tapping your foot to the music, two eighth notes fit into one tap of the foot. That's one eighth note as the foot hits down and one as it comes up.

To get a feeling for how this works, let's take this little Irish children's song. I am going to speak the words in rhythm and then sing them. Just listen first, then rewind the tape. Say the words along with the tape, and sing along too if you'd like.

Mit- ty Mat- ty / had a hen, / she laid eggs for / gen-tle men.

Some-times nine and / some-times ten, / Mit- ty Mat-ty's / fine fat hen.

Repeat the exercise and tap your foot where you see the dashes underneath the words.
Notice where there are two words or syllables for each tap of the foot. These are eighth notes.
Notice where there is just one word for each tap of the foot. These are quarter notes.
Rewind the tape and practice the exercise until you feel comfortable with it. Then learn the tune on the whistle.

MITTY MATTY

children's song

Irish

LESSON FIVE
Sixteenth Notes

Even shorter than the eighth note which gets half a beat, is the sixteenth note which gets one quarter of a beat. This is what sixteenth notes look like:

Sixteenth notes have a double flag on their stem. When sixteenth notes occur next to each other in a tune, they are connected by a double bar.

There are four sixteenth notes for each tap of the foot. Two as the foot goes down and two as it comes up.

The following words were sung to an American fiddle tune in the hills of Pennsylvania many years ago. Listen first, then rewind the tape and speak or sing along with it.

Repeat the exercise and tap your foot where you see the dashes underneath the words.

Notice where there are four syllables for one tap of the foot on the words "John-ny get your." These are sixteenth notes.

Rewind the tape and practice the exercise until you feel comfortable with it. Then learn the tune on the whistle.

JOHNNY GET YOUR HAIR CUT

fiddle tune   American

24

LESSON SIX

Dotted Quarter And Dotted Half Notes

A dot after a note increases that note by one half of its own value.

A regular half note
gets two beats,

A regular quarter note
gets one beat,

whereas a dotted half note
gets three beats.

whereas a dotted quarter note
gets one and a half beats.

This old Scottish air has a dotted quarter and a dotted half note in the second phrase. Let's look at and listen to this phrase by itself.

Rewind the tape and listen again. Tap your foot in time with the quiet click you hear in the background.

Notice how the dotted quarter note (1½ beats) seems elongated compared to the short eighth note (½ beat) that follows it.

Your foot taps twice for the dotted quarter but the eighth note is played just as the foot comes up after the second tap and before it hits down for the third.

The dotted half note gets three full taps of the foot.

Listen to and practice this phrase by itself until you have a feeling for the rhythm. Then learn the piece on the whistle.

THE LYKE WAKE DIRGE

air

Scottish

Dotted Eighth Notes

The figure of a dotted eighth note ♪. followed by a sixteenth note ♪ gives a jaunty swing to a tune. Together they are written like this: ♪.♪

Strictly speaking the dotted eighth note gets 3/4 of a beat, which makes it three times as long as the sixteenth note (1/4 of a beat). But in some styles of music the dotted eighth note is not held so long, nor is the sixteenth note cut so short. The ratio is more like *two* to *one*.

These distinctions are not crucial at this point. Just think of the dotted eighth as getting almost a whole beat and of the sixteenth as coming right before the next beat.

To get an idea of how this sounds let's listen to the charming little Scottish tune *Katie Bairdie*. Rewind the tape and speak or sing the words along with it.

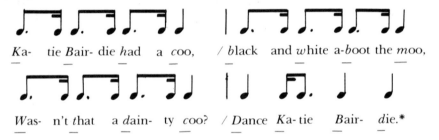

Ka- tie Bair- die *had* a *coo,* / *black* and *white* a-*boot* the *moo,*

Was- n't *that* a *dain-* ty *coo?* / Dance Ka- tie Bair- die.*

Repeat the exercise and tap your foot where you see the dashes underneath the words.

Notice how the first word or syllable in most of the pairs is held long and the second cut short. This is the dotted eighth/sixteenth rhythm.

Notice also how this pattern is reversed on the word "Katie" in line two, giving a quick snap to the tune.

KATIE BAIRDIE

children's song   Scottish

*In Scots "coo" is a cow. "Aboot the moo" means "around the mouth." In verse two on the tape, Katie has a black, fat cat.

6/8 Time

All of the tunes you've learned so far have been in a time signature with a 4 on the bottom in which a quarter note receives one beat. In 6/8 time the note values change. For the 6/8 tunes in this book there are two beats per measure. A beat can be made up of:

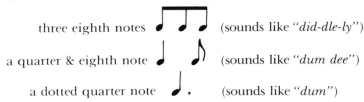

three eighth notes (sounds like *"did-dle-ly"*)

a quarter & eighth note (sounds like *"dum dee"*)

a dotted quarter note (sounds like *"dum"*)

The Anglo-American singing game *Oats and Beans and Barley Grow* is in 6/8 time. It is built on a quarter note / eighth note pattern — a sort of *"dum dee dum dee dum"* rhythm.

Listen first, then rewind the tape and speak or sing along. Repeat the exercise and tap your foot where you see the dashes underneath the words.

First the far-mer /sows his seed, / Then he stands and / takes his ease.

Stamps his feet and /claps his hand and /Looks a-round to / view the land.

OATS AND BEANS AND BARLEY GROW

singing game   Anglo-American

Jigs are lively dance tunes in 6/8 time. They are not confined to Ireland, but are found in England, Scotland and parts of America as well.

This little snippet is perhaps the world's shortest jig. It has quite a few eighth notes in it, which give it that characteristic "diddlely diddlely" Irish jig feeling. Listen first, then proceed as in all other exercises.

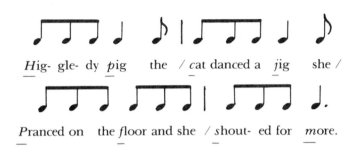

Hig- gle- dy *pig*   the / *cat* danced a *jig*   she /

Pranced on   the *floor* and she / *shout*- ed for   *more.*

Notice again the two strong accents per measure.
Repeat the exercise as necessary and then learn the tune.

THE CAT'S JIG

children's song

Irish

Slurring/High E

Rather than tongue each note in every tune, in some pieces you will want to start to connect the notes for a smoother, less pointed feeling. Connecting the notes is called *slurring* and is not difficult to do.

In the following exercise the notes with the curved line under them are connected. Tongue the *first* note in each pair, but not the second. Listen to the exercise first, then try it yourself.

It is also possible to slur many more than two notes at a time. This will be discussed later in the book on page 53.

Before playing the next piece you will need to learn the note high E — designated with this sign ('). It is fingered the same as low E, but you must blow harder to play it. High E is found in the top space of the staff.

E'

Practice E' and then listen to the next tune, *The Lewis Bridal Song* from Scotland. Learn it with the slurs as given here.

THE LEWIS BRIDAL SONG
bridal song   (also known as Màiri's Wedding)   Scottish

More Notes In The Upper Register

The next tune calls for high F# and G as well as high E all of which will be designated by this sign ('). These notes are fingered the same as their lower counterparts, but to play the higher ones you must blow harder.

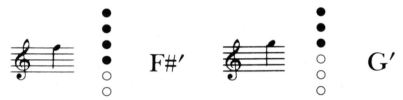

Practice these two notes on your own. Blow as hard as you need to in order to get the notes to jump into the upper register. A good crisp "attack" with the tongue helps.

Identify these notes in the next exercise and then play it. F# is the first letter of *Fine* in Every Good Boy Does Fine. G' simply sits on the top line of the staff.

Now learn the 18th century American marching song *Yankee Doodle*.

YANKEE DOODLE

march   American

The last notes we will learn for now are high A and high B. They are fingered the same as low A and low B, but to play the high notes you must blow harder. Here is how A′ and B′ are written.

Notice that high A has a little line going through it. High B sits on top of the same little line. *These lines are called ledger lines.*

Memorize the position of these notes and practice playing them on your own. If you're not getting them clearly, try a more forceful "attack" with the tongue.

The following tune, a Gaelic Christmas carol from Ireland, uses both these notes.

DON OÍCHE ÚD I MBEITHIL
(That Night in Bethlehem)

Christmas carol   Irish

Congratulations on completing the lessons. These simple tunes have given you the building blocks that the more complex pieces are made of. If you feel as though you need more work at the beginning level, I recommend the excellent book *Tin Whistle For Beginners* by Dona Gilliam and Mizzy McCaskill (see bibliography).

Clarke Tin Whistle Basic Fingerings

○ — open hole　　　● — closed hole　　　◐ — half-covered hole

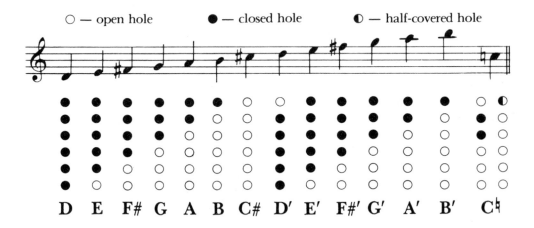

STYLE

As you listen to the rest of the tunes on the tape you will probably notice that the music falls into two basic styles.

In one style just about every note is tongued. This would be appropriate for most English music as well as the American fife tunes.

In the second style most of the notes are slurred. This approach has been traditionally used in Ireland. Some Scottish tunes are also effective when played this way, but with a bit more tonguing.

Ultimately there are no hard and fast rules — each tune should be approached on an individual basis. The renditions on tape can serve as a point of reference, but I encourage you to experiment and find what sounds best to you.

THE TUNES

WALLFLOWERS

children's song

Irish

WHAT SHALL WE DO WITH A DRUNKEN SAILOR?

sea chantey

English

THE QUAKER'S WIFE

jig

Scottish

TIM FINNEGAN'S WAKE

music hall song

Irish

HEY DIDDLE DIS

morris dance

English

THE BONNY, BONNY BROOM

country dance

English

This lovely melody was adapted from the Scots song *The Broom Of The Cowdenknowes.* The air was used as a dance tune in England as early as the 17th century. The piece introduces *cut time* or 2/2 time. Think of this time signature as a fast 4/4 with only two foot taps per measure (each half note gets one beat).

Cut time is indicated by the symbol ₵ . 4/4 or *common time* is indicated by the symbol ₵ .

On The Road To Boston

This old American tune is also known as *General Greene's March*. It is said to have been played by the fifers of Rhode Island General Nathaniel Greene on his way to the siege of Boston in 1775. The melody found its way into the repertoire of New England musicians as an accompaniment to the traditional line or *contra dances* of the region. The dances, and tune, are still going strong after 200 years.

ON THE ROAD TO BOSTON

L'IL LIZA JANE

fiddle tune   American

THE WAGONER'S LAD

song   American

THE EAGLE'S WHISTLE

march   Irish

This Irish bagpipe tune may be well over 300 years old. It has been used as a march, lament, and even a lullaby.

THE PARTING GLASS

song

Irish

As with many slow Irish songs, these note values are not to be strictly followed. Play very freely.

DRUMMOND CASTLE

jig

Scottish

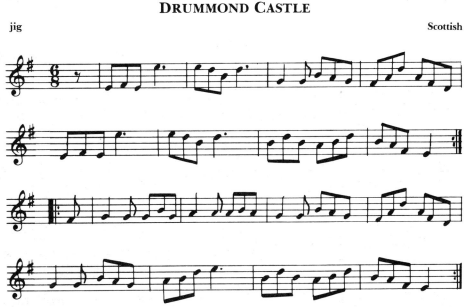

This jig appeared in Neil Gow's collection of 1788. It makes a fine march when played slowly. You will notice this symbol ⁊ at the beginning of the piece. This is an *eighth rest*. In a 6/8 tune it signifies one third of a beat of silence. In a 4/4 tune such as the one on the opposite page, the eighth rest signifies one half beat of silence.

Bonaparte's Grand March

Napoleon Bonaparte was a figure who had a great impact on popular imagination in the 19th century. Many folk tunes of distinct Irish, English and American origin are named after him — *Bonaparte's Advance, Bonaparte's Retreat, Bonaparte Crossing the Rhine, Bonaparte Crossing The Alps,* and *Swaggering Boney* to mention just a few.

The piece below appeared in Captain Francis O'Neill's *Waifs And Strays Of Gaelic Melody* (1922) with the disclaimer that it was *not* a tune of Irish origin. It may be a French composition for fifes or brass band. Whatever its origin, traditional Irish musicians somehow got hold of it and apparently liked it. O'Neill asserts there was no denying the tune's popularity in Ireland in "former times."

BONAPARTE'S GRAND MARCH

*D.C. al Fine means to repeat from the beginning to Fine (Italian for "end").

Morris Dances

These colorful English dances are most associated with the coming of spring and May Day. The morris is not a social dance, but a ceremonial one, performed by a team or *side* with great precision and flair.

Comic characters such as the fool and hobby horse cavort and play pranks on dancers and spectators alike as dancers leap high into the air in what are called *capers*. Each dancer wears dozens of tiny bells sewn to a sort of legging. The effect of hundreds of these bells all jingling in time to the music can be very striking.

A favorite accompaniment for the morris was the pipe and tabor, a three-hole flute and drum combination (see p. 47). When this tradition waned, instruments such as the fiddle and melodeon became popular. Tin whistles accompanied by side drums are known to have been used on occasion.

Morris music is played quite slowly but with a strong rhythm.

THE BLUE-EYED STRANGER

morris dance   English

THE LADIES' PLEASURE

morris dance

English

In the third part of *The Ladies' Pleasure* the music switches to longer notes which gives the effect of the tune slowing down to half speed. This section is for the dancers' capers. The few measures of 3/8 time have one beat each. Listen carefully to the tape to get the feel of this.

IDBURY HILL

morris dance

English

41

THE BOATMAN

English

A very old tune, this first appeared in Playford's *Dancing Master* in 1651. Whistle players may wish to omit the short note at the end of the third line for breathing purposes.

THE TRIP TO TUNBRIDGE

country dance

English

This fine tune appeared in the book *Kentish Hops* in 1793. An F natural (F ♮) occurs in the first measure of the fourth line of the piece. To play this note, simply start on the note E and straighten R2 at the first joint so that the F# (second hole) is half uncovered. This will give you an F ♮. If you wish to omit this note, substitute G′ or D′ for it.

Quick Scotch

Better known as *The Fairy Dance*, this tune was something of an "international hit" in the early 19th century. Originally a Scots reel attributed to Nathaniel Gow (1763-1831), variants of it pop up in England, Ireland, Wales, The Isle of Man and America under many different titles.

Fifers in the U.S. Army adopted this reel for camp duty and called it *Quick Scotch*, replacing an older tune of the same name. Camp duty tunes regulated every aspect of an enlisted man's daily routine — when to get up, when to eat, and when to go to sleep. A lively strain such as *Quick Scotch* would be used to rouse him out of bed in the morning.

Fiddlers in the southern Appalachians also played a version of this tune, but they called it *Old Molly Hare* and sang these words to the second part:

> Old Molly Hare, whatcha doin' there?
> Sittin' by the fireside smokin' a cigar.

QUICK SCOTCH

THE GAY GORDONS

couple dance

Scottish

THE OLD GREY CAT

reel

English

44   Play C# where the sharp signs occur.

RUFTY TUFTY

country dance   arranged by Marshall Barron   English

This tune is a duet. The harmony part is on the lower of the two staves. The piece was first published in Playford's *Dancing Master* in 1651.

Notice that the second part of the tune has a *first and second ending.* Play what's under bracket 1 the first time through and skip what's under bracket 2. On the repeat play only what's under bracket 2.

45

High C#, D And Third Octave Notes

Most tin whistle tunes stay within the range of D to B'. But there are other notes which can be played on the instrument. High C# and High D complete the second octave of notes. They are fingered like their lower counterparts and are written like this:

Try these notes in the following tune.

LADS-A-BUNCHUM

morris dance   English

Third octave notes are rarely played because of their shrillness. But they do have their use outdoors, in large spaces, or in noisy situations.

I would strongly advise anyone interested in learning these notes to wear some kind of hearing protection — preferably ear plugs.

E'' can be fingered identically to its lower counterparts, but to get F#'' and G'' cleanly, cover the bottom hole of the whistle with R3.

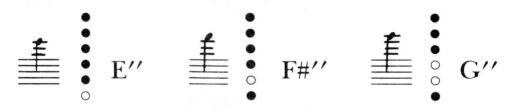

Because third octave notes are difficult to read with the numerous ledger lines, we will notate the music an octave lower with the symbol *8 va* at the beginning of each tune. *8 va* means to play one octave higher than written.

Pipe And Tabor Tunes

Playing in the third octave has its precedent in traditional English music, as this was the range of the high-pitched *three-hole pipe*, known in England as early as the 13th century. By using a series of overtones a player could produce at least 11 or 12 notes from the three holes. This was enough for simple dance tunes and it left one hand free to beat out rhythms on a drum called a *tabor*. Together as the *pipe and tabor* the two instruments formed an economical one-man dance band particularly favored for morris dancing. (See illustrations pp. 40 & 50).

Note the curved line connecting the two E's in the first measure of line three. When a curved line connects two notes of the same pitch it is called a *tie* and means to play the two notes as one long note.

I'LL GO AND ENLIST FOR A SAILOR

morris dance

English

CONSTANT BILLY

morris dance

English

The best method of playing C ♮ ′ is half covering the top hole. See fingering chart on inside back cover for an alternate method.

Fife Tunes

The character of fife music lends itself well to being played in the third octave on the tin whistle. Since the fife was a military instrument played outdoors for marching and signalling, it had to be sounded in its upper register for maximum carrying power.

GOVERNOR KING'S MARCH

march

American

THE BOSTON MARCH

arranged by John C. Moon

march

Another duet. Originally from Joshua Cushing's *Fifer's Companion,* circa 1804.

THE GIRL I LEFT BEHIND ME

English/Irish/American

march

Kemps nine daies vvonder.

Performed in a daunce from
London to Norwich.

*Containing the pleafure, paines and hinde entertainment
of William Kemp betweene London and that Citty
in his late Morrice.*

*Wherein is fomewhat fet downe worth note ; to reprooue
the flaunders fpred of him : many things merry,
nothing hurtfull.*

Written by himfelfe to fatisfie his friends.

LONDON
Printed by *E. A.* for *Nicholas Ling*, and are to be
folde at his fhop at the weft doore of Saint
Paules Church 1600.

Kemp's Jig

Will Kemp was a comic actor in Elizabethan England and a colleague of Shakespeare. He is also remembered for what was surely one of the great publicity stunts of the late 16th century — *dancing* from London to Norwich, a distance of almost 100 miles, in *9 days*! Kemp performed the feat in 1599 and gave an account of it in a pamphlet, *Kemps Nine Daies Wonder*, published the next year.

The tune below may well be one he danced to on that muddy pot-holed road almost 400 years ago. The piece was preserved in an old lute manuscript in the Cambridge University Library.

KEMP'S JIG

The Helston Furry

Celebrating the arrival of May has long been an important tradition in England dating back to times when people believed that certain rites had to be followed in order to ensure the fertility of the fields for the coming year.

Many wonderful customs existed to usher in the spring. One of the most noteworthy survivals comes from the town of Helston in Cornwall. There a select group of townspeople dress in formal attire and dance through the entire town in a long serpentine procession. The dancers wend their way not only through streets, but also through houses — in the front door and out the back.

At one time the procession had elements of a spring cleaning or purification rite, as dancers carried sprigs of May blossoms with which they brushed various objects as they passed through the houses. Local legend also has it that the dance originated as a device to scare away the devil!

The procession still takes place annually on May 8th, Old May Day or *Furry Day* as it is called — from the Latin *feria* meaning holiday. The tune below is the traditional favorite for the Furry dance.

AN ENGLISH MAYPOLE

OVER THE WATERFALL

fiddle tune   American

I have yet to come across evidence of tin whistles being played in the Southern Appalachians. Some of the fiddle tunes from the area do adapt nicely to the whistle.

WEST FORK GALS

fiddle tune   American

Ornamentation In Irish Music

Irish tin whistle playing draws on a rich wind instrument tradition with roots in the bagpiping of the 16th and 17th centuries. A bagpiper cannot tongue to articulate notes since there is no direct contact between the player's mouth and the chanter, the part of the instrument playing the tune. Pipers overcome this difficulty by deftly flicking their fingers to introduce tiny little *grace notes* into the music.

These grace notes have the aural effect of separating the main melody notes. Sometimes grace notes are combined into more complex flourishes called *ornaments* which not only help separate the notes, but add color and interest to the tune.

Irish tin whistle players have traditionally followed a piper's approach to the music, connecting most of the melody notes and introducing grace notes with the fingers. Some players avoid tonguing almost entirely, while others use it here and there for effect. In either case the overall impression is one of a great stream of notes decorated with little flourishes.

What follows is a necessarily condensed introduction to Irish tin whistle ornamentation. Whole books could be and have been written on the subject.

****

Before proceeding any further it is important to note that there is no need to ornament most of the tunes in this book. The particular pieces chosen sound attractive *with or without* ornaments.

All but advanced players would be wise to avoid the more complex ornaments for a few years and instead concentrate on developing a solid foundation of good rhythm and phrasing.

Slurring (Review)

To prepare for the work on ornamentation, let's review *slurring* or connecting the notes. Try playing a scale without tonguing at all.

You may find this difficult to do at first if you are used to tonguing, but it actually is easier than articulating each note. It's just a question of getting accustomed to a new way of doing things.

Try the following exercise. Remember to connect all the notes over the curved line. Tongue only the first note in each group to be slurred.

Cuts

Until now if you've wanted to make two G's on the whistle you've just tongued them. The piper's way of playing two G's is to quickly flick the left ring finger (L3) which has the effect of *"cutting"* the two notes from each other. Listen to the example on tape and then try this grace note or cut for yourself.

Notice how the cut is written as a tiny slashed note in between the two melody notes. It should be barely audible, so don't lift your finger very high.

Here are the basic cuts used by most whistle players:

Use the A finger (L3) to cut the melody notes D through G. This is designated by a tiny note either in the second space from the bottom of the staff or above the staff with a ledger line through it.

Use the C finger (L1) to cut the melody notes A and B. This is designated by a tiny note in the third space of the staff.

Try the following scale with the cuts as marked. Play without tonguing.

(Grace notes can also be introduced on the notes C# and D', but this is a more advanced technique than what we should be working on at the moment.)

The following Irish polka, a lively dance in 2/4 time, uses some of the cuts you've just learned. As an exercise, try to play the piece *without any tonguing* at all. In Irish tin whistle music slurs are generally not notated, as it is assumed that the player will connect the notes according to his or her own taste.

polka　　　　**TARMON'S POLKA**　　　　Irish

More Cuts

In the previous examples we've been using cuts to separate two notes of the same pitch. Cuts can also be used for *accent* between *two notes of different pitches* as in the example below.

Listen to this on tape and then try it for yourself. Notice that you use the A finger (L3) to do the cut.

Make sure that you lift your cutting finger before making the note to be accented. Don't lower it until you've moved the other finger (or fingers) necessary to make the next note. This will give your grace notes a clean sound.

Here is a scale with cuts used for accent. Again we will use the A finger (L3) for the notes D through G and the C finger (L1) for the notes A and B.

Here are some cuts going down the scale. Note that in this exercise you will have to cut the G with the C finger (L1).

Various types of cuts figure into the next tune, another polka. Play it slowly like a march at first and don't use any tonguing — let your fingers do all the work.

TRALEE GAOL

polka

Irish

Strikes

Another method of separating two identical notes without tonguing is a grace note called a *strike* or *tip*.

This movement involves hitting the hole of the note to be ornamented with the next lowest finger. In the example below, play G then quickly hit the third hole from the bottom of the whistle with the right index finger (R1). Listen first, then try it.

The ornament is notated as a tiny grace note one step in pitch *below* the melody note. Strikes can be done on any note (except D) by hitting with the next lowest finger.

The next tune is a *slip jig*, a very graceful dance in 9/8 time. The slip jig has 3 beats per measure — a sort of *diddlely, diddlely, diddlely* feel to it. This particular slip jig was originally a *dandling song* for bouncing a baby on the knee. Use the tongue sparingly and add the cuts and strikes as notated.

THE LITTLE FAIR CANNAVANS

slip jig   Irish

Rolls

The most distinctive feature of Irish tin whistle ornamentation is a figure called the *roll*. This is simply a combination of a cut and a strike. The *long roll* is most often used in jigs where three eighth notes of identical pitch may need to be separated. Listen to this example on tape.

Let's break this movement down into three steps:

1. Play the note G.
2. Cut the G with the A finger (L3).
3. Strike the G with the F# finger (R1).*

Rewind the tape and listen to it again, then practice this ornament yourself. Make sure that the strike is crisp and that you blow continuously throughout the roll. You may wish to tongue the initial melody note of the roll for extra accent.

An almost universally adopted method of notating the roll is the "half moon" sign which looks like this:

It gives the tune a less "notey" appearance and we will use it in this book.

When you have some idea of how to do a G roll, listen to and try the next piece of music, an old piping jig whose title translates as *Wise Nora*.

It may be played without rolls by substituting the notes GAG for the ornament. You may add other cuts or articulation if you wish.

NÓRA CRÍONA

jig   Irish

* Two fingers, R1 and R2, may be used to strike simultaneously. If done lightly this can be very effective.

Reels

The reel originated in Scotland sometime in the 18th century. This type of tune eventually became a mainstay of the Irish repertoire, surpassing all other forms of dance music in popularity.

Reels are played in cut time with two strong accents per measure. The tempo can be quite fast, although this is not always the case. Before going on to a more complex reel with ornaments here are two simpler examples for you to try.

ROLLING IN THE RYEGRASS

reel   Irish

THE BOYS OF 25

reel   Irish

Rolls In Reels

The roll you learned in *Nóra Críona* also occurs quite often in reels. The only difference is that the first of the three eighth notes is no longer on an accented beat as in the jig. Listen to the following example and then try it.

This type of roll is an integral part of the structure of the following tune. The piece also has one other new element which you will see frequently in this type of music — the triplet. A triplet is simply three quick notes played in the space of two. It is notated with a small 3 over or under the music. The nonsense syllables "did-dle-ly" best capture the rhythm of the triplet. Listen to the following example then try it yourself.

Now try the tune. Though reels are often played quite fast, go over this one slowly at first to get a feeling for the ornaments.

KITTY'S GONE A MILKING

reel   Irish

Short Rolls

The *short roll* is used for extra emphasis on an accented beat. The movement is done with the same fingers as the preceding rolls, but is executed more rapidly.

Listen to the example of the short roll on tape, then try it yourself following these steps:

1. Have your fingers in position to play G *but do not blow*.
2. Raising the A finger (L3) blow to make a quick cut on G.
3. Flick the right index finger (R1) to make a quick strike on G.

Practice slowly at first, then try to pick up speed. When done up to speed the short roll sounds like a burst or cluster of crisp little notes before the accented note. To convey this effect it would probably be best notated like this:

We will again use the standard half moon sign to make the music look less "notey."

The following tune is a *fling*, an Irish adaptation of the Scots strathspey. It is normally played at a moderate speed, which should help you to work in the short rolls. The tune may also be played omitting the rolls entirely.

MAGGIE PICKENS

fling

Irish

Crans

The *cran* is a classic ornament on the uilleann pipes, Ireland's distinctive bellows blown bagpipe. The movement consists of three D's or E's separated out by three cuts. The fingers used are A, G, and F# (L3, R1 & R2).

 also notated as

To do a cran follow these steps:

1. Put your fingers in position to play low D, but do not blow.
2. Raise the A finger (L3) and blow to make the first cut on D.
3. Cut with R1.
4. Cut with R2.

Start slowly at first. *The secret is to replace one finger before lifting the next.* This makes for a crisp sounding cran.

(N.B. In the tune that follows, the last cran in each part has no A grace note. Simply play the note D, then cut with R1 and R2.)

FRAHER'S JIG

jig   Irish

That touches on most of the ornaments used in Irish whistle playing. The roll, cut, and strike can be done on almost any note and are used in a variety of ways. There are other advanced techniques such as double cut rolls and short crans. For those wishing to study ornamentation more thoroughly, the *Tutor For the Feadóg Stáin* by Micheál Ó hAlmhain and Séamus MacMathúna is highly recommended.

For the rest of the book, I have only notated ornaments where they are really essential to the structure of a tune. However I've played the tunes on the tape as a traditional player would, adding ornaments to the basic version where it seems appropriate. I've used all of the ornaments we've covered in the text, as well as some of the more advanced techniques.

But as stated at the beginning of the section, most of the tunes can be played without ornaments and should be played this way until you are really comfortable with the music.

A Note About Breathing

Breathing for Irish (and other) tunes can sometimes pose a challenge as many pieces in the repertoire were not originally composed on wind instruments and are full of short, fast notes. The fiddler doesn't have to think about where to breathe. When playing a fiddle tune, a tin whistler may have to use some ingenuity to find a place to breathe that won't spoil the effect of the tune.

As a general rule, *don't breathe between short notes.*

Look for a long note to shorten and take your breath there.

However in some tunes there aren't many long notes. In this case the traditional Irish whistle player drops out a short note and substitutes a breath for it. There are certain patterns that are favored for doing this, such as dropping out the middle eighth note in a group of three in a jig or the second eighth note in a group of four in a reel. Listen to these examples on tape.

You will discover more about how this is done by listening carefully to traditional players.

Hornpipes

Hornpipe is the name of an old reed instrument that was literally a pipe with a cow's horn at one end. The horn's function was similar to that of the bell of a trumpet.

The hornpipe gave its name to a dance that originated in England and spread from there throughout the isles and America. The dance was popular on stage in the 18th and 19th centuries — its association with sailors may have originally been more theatrical than nautical.

The style of playing this type of dance tune varies considerably from place to place. In general hornpipes are played at a moderate speed with a jaunty swing. Though often written as undotted eighth notes, it is assumed that the performer will make the odd eighth notes about twice as long as the even ones.

The two pieces below, though probably of English origin, adapt themselves nicely to the Irish style of ornamentation.

THE DURHAM RANGERS

THE STEAMBOAT HORNPIPE

Poll Hapenny

This Irish hornpipe is an excellent example of how a tune gets reshaped as it is handed down orally from generation to generation.

The piece began its life as *Molly Macalpin,* a stately composition for harp that was probably intended as a song of praise to a noblewoman. As the air passed into the oral tradition of the peasantry, the tune easily became a hornpipe, which in Ireland is often played quite slowly to accommodate the intricate steps of the dancers.

And while the melody and rhythm underwent changes, so did the title. Molly became Polly, Macalpin became Halpin and then in the neatest twist of all, Halpin somehow became Hapenny — short for *halfpenny,* a small coin then in circulation. So humble *Poll Hapenny* she is to this day.

The original piece, *Molly Macalpin,* first appeared in print in the 1796 edition of Edward Bunting's *General Collection of the Ancient Irish Music.*

POLL HAPENNY

SCATTERY ISLAND SLIDE

slide

Irish

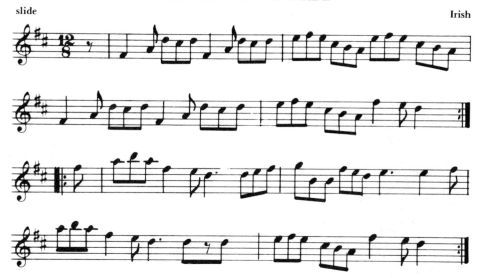

Slides are very lively dance tunes in 12/8 time. They have four strong accents per measure.

MAURICE MANLEY'S POLKA

polka

Irish

RYAN'S SLIP JIG

slip jig

Irish

Strathspeys

The strathspey is the type of tune that the Highland fling is danced to. It is named for the district around the valley of the river Spey in Scotland. The strathspey's distinct and spirited rhythm makes great use of the sixteenth note followed by the dotted eighth, a figure sometimes called the *"Scotch snap"*. The feeling of this is best captured by the syllables *duh-DEE*.

The two strathspeys that follow are both excellent for dancing. The first is best known as a *puirt a beul* (literally "mouth music"), a Gaelic nonsense song for dancing. Its subject is watery oatmeal — the title translates as *"thin gruel."*

The second is a very old pipe tune which has been the vehicle for many lyrics, including *Katie Bairdie* on p. 26.

BROCHAN LOM

strathspey

Scottish

WILL YOU GO TO SHERIFF MUIR?

strathspey

Scottish

HOT PUNCH

march/jig

Scottish

BALMORAL CASTLE

strathspey

Scottish

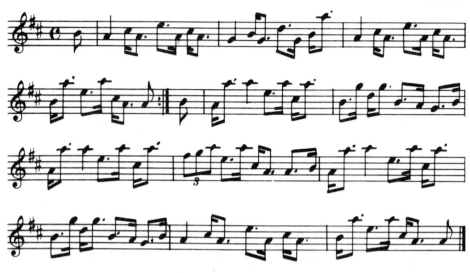

THE KILT IS MY DELIGHT

reel

Scottish

THE OYSTER WIVES' RANT

reel

Scottish

The Muckin' O' Geordie's Byre

This lively Scots tune in 6/8 time is a great favorite to march or dance to. The melody is from a comical song in Lowland Scots dialect whose title translates as "The Cleaning of Geordie's Cow Barn."

Lowland Scots is a variant of the early language of North Britain, sprinkled with many old and unusal terms no longer understood by most speakers of modern English.

Below is the original chorus of the song, with a translation in footnote:
"The graip was tint, the besom was deen,
The barra widna row its leen.
O siccan a sarsies never was seen
At the muckin' o' Geordie's byre."*

THE MUCKIN' O' GEORDIE'S BYRE

jig/march

Scottish

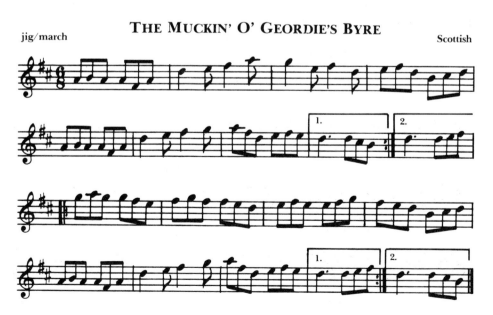

*" The pitch fork was bent, the broom was worn out. / The wheelbarrow wouldn't roll by itself. / And such a predicament never was seen, / At the cleaning of Geordie's cow barn."

OLD CAPE BRETON MARCH

march

Scottish

2/4 marches are a very important category of tune on the Highland bagpipe. Because of the dotted rhythms in these tunes, a new note, the *thirty-second note*, is used in conjunction with the dotted sixteenth note. The thirty-second note is written with three flags and receives an eighth of a beat. All this tends to make 2/4 marches look quite intimidating at first, but if you just think of this tune as having a "swing" somewhat related to the hornpipe or strathspey and let the tape help you, you'll probably find it quite accessible. This particular march comes from the fiddle repertoire of Cape Breton Island, Nova Scotia.

CUTTY'S WEDDING

strathspey

Scottish

CION A' BHUNTÀTA
(Scarce O'Tatties)

jig   Scottish

A recently composed tune by Norman Maclean, piper from Uist in the Outer Hebrides. A friend of his working in London complained about the quality of potatoes there, and so this tune was born. The piece sounds best on the whistle when played with rolls. Cut the E & F rolls with L3, the A roll with L1. Strike with the finger directly below the main note of each roll.

MARCHING THE SOLDIER ALONG

march   Irish

This is an unusual two-part Irish version of a longer Scottish march known as *The 79th's Farewell To Gibraltar*. This variant comes from County Mayo, Ireland, perhaps brought over by migrant workers back from the harvest in Scotland. It is played somewhat like a hornpipe.

Slow Airs

Amongst the most beautiful music in the Irish tradition are slow airs adapted from old style Gaelic singing. These tend to be very free in rhythm and meter, so the transcriptions given here are only an approximation of what is being played. It would be best to use your ears as a guide for this.

CASADH AN TSÚGÁIN
(The Twisting of the Hayrope)

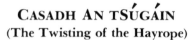

ÚIR-CHILL A' CHREAGÁIN
(The Clay of Cill Creggan)

FOR THE SAKES OF OLD DECENCY

reel

Irish

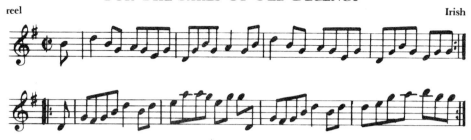

JIM WARD'S JIG

jig

Irish

Another fairly recent tune, this jig was composed by the late Jim Ward of Milltown Malbay, County Clare. R.I.P.

ROLLING IN THE BARRELL

reel

Irish

THE BOY THAT SHAVED HIS FATHER

reel   Irish

JOHNNY MICKEY'S

polka   Irish

EGAN'S POLKA

polka   Irish

PIGTOWN

reel   Irish

THE LITTLE BAG OF SPUDS

reel   Irish

SEÁN SA CHEO
(John in the Fog)

reel   Irish

75

Appendix

THE MUFFIN MAN

d g g a/ b g g f#/ e a a g/ f# d d/
d g g a/ b g g f#/ e a f#/ d/ g //

EXERCISE IN LESSON TWO

g a b c/ d' c b a/
g b d' b/ g //

ORANGES & LEMONS

d' b d'/ b g a b/ c a d'/ b g/
d' b d'/ g a b/ c a d'/ g//

GO TELL AUNT RHODY

f# f# e/ d d/ e e g/ f# e d/
a a g/ f# f# f#/ e d e f#/ d//

MITTY MATTY

g b g b/ g b d'/ f# a f# a/ f# a c /
g b g b/ g b d'/ c a f# a/ b g g //

JOHNNY GET YOUR HAIR CUT

g b a g e d/ e d e d/ g b a g e d/ e f# g //

PHRASE IN LESSON SIX

b a b a/ f# //

THE LYKE WAKE DIRGE

e d e/ g f# e e/ b a b a/ f# f#/
g g f# a/ g f# e f# d/ e g a f#/ e //

KATIE BAIRDIE

a b a g f#/ g a/ e f# g f# e f# g/
a b a g f#/ g a/ d f# a e d //

OATS AND BEANS AND BARLEY GROW

b b b a/ g g g/ c c c b/ a a a/
b c d' c /b c d' b/ a c b a/ g g g//

THE CAT'S JIG

b g g g a/ b a b d' b/ c b c a d' c /
b g g g / /

EXERCISE IN LESSON NINE

d e f# g/ a g f# /
e b e f#/ d d //

THE LEWIS BRIDAL SONG

d e d e/ g a b/ a g e g/ b a b d'/
d e d e/ g a b/ a g e g/ d d //
d' e' d' e'/ d c b/ a g e g/ b a b d'/
d' e' d' e'/ d c b/ a g e g/ d d//

EXERCISE IN LESSON TEN

d' e' f# g'/ f#' e' d' a /
d' f#' e' g'/ f#' e' d' //

YANKEE DOODLE

d' d' e' f#'/ d' f#' e' a/ d' d' e' f#'/d'
c#/
d' d' e' f#'/ g' f#' e' d'/ c# a b c#'/d'
d' //
b c# b a/ b c# d'/ a b a g/ f# a/
b c# b a/ b c# d' b/ a d' c# e'/ d' d' //

DON OÍCHE ÚD I mBEITHIL

e'/ a c b a/ g a a/ c d' e' d' b/ g e/
a c b a/ g a a/ c d' e' b a/ a e'/
g' e' d' e' /g' a' b' a'/ g' e' d' c d'/ e'
e'/
a c b a/ g a a/ c d' e' b a/ a //

Transposing

Some tin whistles are *transposing instruments*. What this means is that the notes that are written on the page are not actually the same notes that sound when the whistle is being played. The Clarke tin whistle which comes with this book is actually pitched in "C". When all fingers are down it sounds a C even though we are calling this note D and writing it as a D.

This can be quite puzzling and seemingly absurd to a newcomer to music. Why not just write the music in C? It's a very logical question.

There is a good answer for it though. Some wind instruments exist in families which include different sized members of different pitches. As a convenience, the terminology of all the instruments is standardized so that the player only needs to learn one set of names for the fingerings.

At present there are at least six different pitched tin whistles available. Learning six different names for each hole and finger position would be rather confusing. To simplify matters the bottom note of the whistle is always called D regardless of its actual pitch. The music comes out sounding perfectly fine on whatever whistle you play — it's just higher or lower depending on the length of the instrument.

Since most tin whistle, fife and fiddle books are written in D and related keys, this nomenclature gives you immediate access to a whole range of musical literature suitable to the instrument.

The only place where you may run into problems is when you go to play with other people. Then you have to make some adjustments.

PLAYING WITH OTHER INSTRUMENTS

If you are playing in a big music session in which everyone else is playing in the *actual* key of D — not *nominal* D — then you need to have a whistle actually pitched in D. Fortunately there are several different brands of these available.* You should get one for such situations.

However in a small group, especially amongst friends, some very interesting combinations can be worked out using your C whistle. You will have to ask the other musicians to play the music one step lower than it is written. For some musicians this is no problem, as they are used to doing it all the time.

One traditional practice that bears mentioning is tuning a fiddle down one whole step. The fiddler can then play along reading the notes as written, but the fiddle will actually be in tune with your C whistle.

There are examples of this on the tape, as well as examples of the whistle being played with an old style *melodeon* (accordion) and different types of percussion. The percussion includes tambourine, snare drum, *bodhrán* (an Irish goatskin frame drum) and bones. (The bones are actually rib bones of a sheep that are clacked together with a vigorous motion of the wrist to produce different rhythms.)

And of course you can play with other Clarke tin whistles. One of the nicest combinations of all is a few whistles with the right percussion.

---

*The Clarke Company is as of this writing preparing to re-introduce a D-pitched whistle into production.

BIBLIOGRAPHY

Quite a literature on playing the tin whistle has emerged in the last 20 years. The following listing is by no means complete. Addresses of publishers are listed only where there may be some difficulty obtaining the books from the sources listed on the next page.

An asterisk next to a book means that it is devoted solely to Irish music. A dagger next to a book means that it is accompanied by a recording. *A whistle actually pitched in D is necessary to play with the recordings.*

TIN WHISTLE BOOKS

BEGINNERS
Gilliam, D. & McCaskill, M., *Tin Whistle For Beginners*, Mel Bay Publications
Loane, Brian, *How To Play The Tin Whistle*, Universal Editions, 2/3 Fareham St., Dean St., London, W1V 4DU, England
†*Vallely, B. & E., *Fifty Simple Tunes For The Tin Whistle*, Armagh Pipers Club, 83 Mullacreevie Park, Armagh, Co. Armagh, No. Ireland

INTERMEDIATE
†*Cotter, Geraldine, *Traditional Irish Tin Whistle Tutor*, Ossian Publications
† Gilliam, D. & McCaskill, M., *The Whistler's Pocket Companion*, Mel Bay Publications
Williamson, Robin, *The Pennywhistle Book*, Oak Publications

ADVANCED
†*McCullough, L.E., *The Complete Irish Tin Whistle Tutor*, Music Sales Corporation
† *Ó hAlmhain, M. & MacMathúna, S., *Tutor For The Feadóg Stáin*, Comhaltas Ceoltóirí Eireann, Belgrave Sq., Monkstown, Co. Dublin, Ireland

COLLECTIONS OF MUSIC

For advanced players there are literally hundreds of books of fiddle, fife, and bagpipe tunes most of which can be played on the tin whistle. Some basic titles are suggested below.

AMERICAN
Bayard, Samuel, *Dance To The Fiddle, March To The Fife: Instrumental Folk Tunes in Pennsylvania*, The Pennsylvania State University Press
Miller, R. & Perron, J., *New England Fiddler's Repertoire*, Fiddlecase Books
Sweet, Ralph, *The Fifer's Delight*, Sweetheart Flute Company

ENGLISH
Karpeles, M. & Schofield, K., *100 English Folk Dance Airs*, Hargail Music Press
Northumbrian Pipers' Society, *The First and Second Northumbian Pipers' Tune Books*, (The address of the Honorable Secretary of the society may be obtained from Newcastle Information Centre, City Library, Newcastle upon Tyne, England)
Raven, Michael, *1,000 English Country Dance Tunes*, Michael Raven Publications, 26 Church Lane, Derrington, Stafford, England

IRISH
Breathnach, Breandan, *Ceol Rince na hEireann (The Dance Music of Ireland, 3 volumes)*, An Gúm
O'Neill, Francis, *O'Neill's Music Of Ireland*, Rock Chapel Press
Roche, Francis, *The Roche Collection Of Traditional Irish Music*, Ossian Publications

SCOTTISH
Carlin, Richard, *The Gow Collection Of Scottish Dance Music*, Oak Publications
MacDonald, Keith N., *The Skye Collection Of The Best Reels & Strathspeys*, Skye Collection, P.O. Box 30, Whitney Pier P.S., Sydney, Nova Scotia, Canada, B1N 3B1
Robertson, Donald Struan, *Scots Guards Standard Settings Of Pipe Music*, Paterson's Publications Ltd., 36 Wigmore St., London, W.1.

INDEX